FROM PUPPY TO DOG

Anita Ganeri

www.heinemann.co.uk/library
Visit our website to find out more information about Heinemann Library books.

To order:
 Phone 44 (0) 1865 888066
 Send a fax to 44 (0) 1865 314091
 Visit the Heinemann Bookshop at www.heinemann.co.uk/library to browse our catalogue and order online.

First published in Great Britain by Heinemann Library, Halley Court, Jordan Hill, Oxford OX2 8EJ, part of Harcourt Education. Heinemann is a registered trademark of Harcourt Education Ltd.

Editorial: Nancy Dickmann and Sarah Chappelow
Design: Ron Kamen and edesign
Picture Research: Ruth Blair and Kay Altwegg
Production: Helen McCreath

Originated by Modern Age
Printed and bound in China by South China Printing Company

ISBN 0 431 05073 2
10 09 08 07 06
10 9 8 7 6 5 4 3 2 1

The British Library Cataloguing in Publication Data
Ganeri, Anita
From puppy to dog. - (How living things grow)
571.8'19772
A full catalogue record for this book is available from the British Library.

Acknowledgements
The Publishers would like to thank the following for permission to reproduce the following photographs: Alamy pp. **17** (Image State), **24, 25**; Ardea pp. **6** (John Daniels), **7** (John Daniels), **8** (John Daniels), **11** (John Daniels), **14** (John Daniels), **23** (John Daniels); Corbis pp. **4, 5** (Ronnie Kaufman), **10, 15, 16** (LWA/Dann Tardif); FLPA pp. **18** (Brian Turner), **19** (Foto Natura Catalogue), **20** (Roland Abspoel/Foto Natura), **22** (Mitsuaki Iwago/Minden Pictures), **26** (Roger Wilmshurst), **27** (Foto Natura Stock); Getty Images pp. **9, 21** (National Geographic); Photolibrary.com pp. **12, 13, 29**.

Cover photograph of a dog reproduced with permission of Alamy Images/Stockbyte.

Illustrations: Martin Sanders

Every effort has been made to contact copyright holders of any material reproduced in this book. Any omissions will be rectified in subsequent printings if notice is given to the publishers. The paper used to print this book comes from sustainable resources.

Contents

Words written in bold, **like this**, are explained in the glossary.

Have you ever seen a dog?

A dog is a kind of animal called a **mammal**. People keep dogs as pets. Wild dogs live in some parts of the world.

*There are many different types of dog. This dog is a **female** golden retriever.*

4

Golden retrievers have a long coat, floppy ears, and a long tail.

You are going to learn how a golden retriever is born, grows up, has babies, gets old, and dies. This is the dog's life cycle.

What is a baby dog called?

5

A new litter

A baby dog is called a puppy. The puppy starts life in her mother's body. She grows and grows. After nine weeks, she is ready to be born.

This dog has puppies growing inside her tummy.

6

The mother dog may have six to eight puppies. They are born one after the other. These puppies are called a **litter**.

These puppies are so small you could hold one in your hand.

Newborn puppies

The puppy is tiny and helpless. She cannot see or hear. But she can smell. She uses smell to stay close to her mother.

The puppy needs her mother to take care of her.

Grooming helps the mother show the puppy that she is safe.

The **female** dog looks after her puppies. She feeds the puppies and licks their fur. This licking is called **grooming**.

What does the puppy eat?

9

Growing fast

The puppy feeds on her mother's milk. The milk is full of **nutrients**. The nutrients help the puppy to grow.

*The puppy has to find a **teat** to drink from.*

10

The puppy can look around.

When she is about ten days old, the puppy's eyes open. She can see. A few days later, her ears start to open. She can hear.

What does the puppy do?

11

Play and sleep

The puppy plays with her brothers and sisters. They pretend to fight each other. This shows them which puppy is the strongest.

The puppies can bark and wag their tails.

12

Puppies need sleep to help them grow.

The puppies quickly get tired. They flop down in a heap. They fall asleep. The puppies sleep a lot.

Visit to the vet

The puppy is about two months old. She is taken to the **vet**. The vet gives her an **injection**.

The injection stops the puppy getting **diseases**.

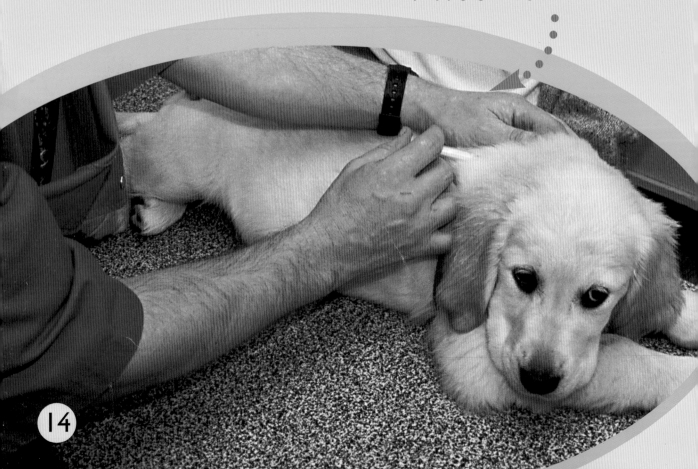

The vet also checks that the puppy is healthy.

After her injection, the puppy can go outside.

How long does the puppy stay with her mother? 15

Leaving mother

The puppy is about three months old. She is growing fast. Now she is old enough to leave her mother. She goes to a new home.

The puppy's brothers and sisters will all go to different homes.

16

The puppy can run fast now.

The puppy needs lots of **exercise**. Her new owner takes her for walks. Exercise helps the puppy's muscles to grow stronger.

When is the puppy grown up?

17

Grown-up dog

The puppy is about a year and a half old. She is fully grown. She does not drink milk any more. She eats meat and biscuits.

Meat and biscuits make the dog's teeth strong and keep her healthy.

Dogs are good swimmers.

The young dog can be trained to chase balls or sticks. She brings them back to her owner.

When can the dog have puppies?

Having puppies

The dog is fully grown. She can have her own puppies. Her owner takes her to meet a **male** dog. The male and **female** dogs **mate**.

Dogs sniff each other when they meet.

*A new **litter** of puppies has arrived.*

The puppies grow inside the female dog's tummy. They are born about nine weeks later. Then the dog's life cycle starts again.

21

Caring for the puppies

The dog feeds her puppies on milk. This is what her mother did for her. She looks after the puppies for about three months. Then the puppies go to new homes.

These puppies are nearly ready to go to a new home.

The new owners makes sure their puppy is healthy.

The new owner looks after the puppy. The owner makes sure the puppy has food, water, and lots of **exercise**.

Staying healthy

The dog is about five years old.
She is fit and healthy. She has a
thick, **glossy** coat. Her tail is long
and waggy.

*A young dog needs lots of **exercise**.*

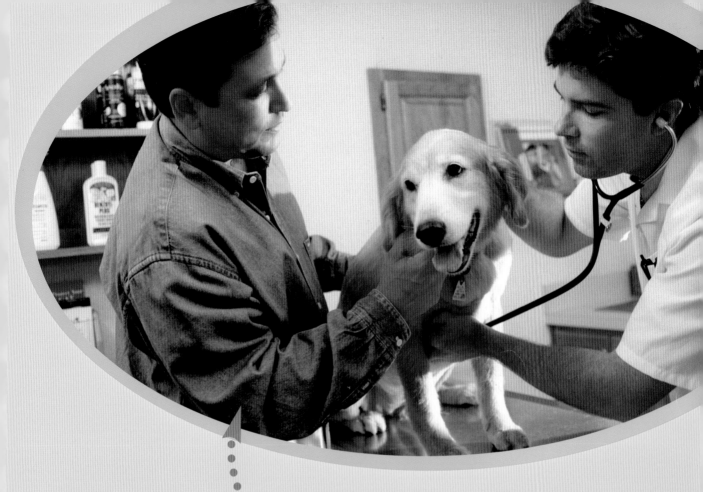

*A **vet** can give the dog medicine to make her better.*

As the dog gets older, she sometimes gets ill. She might stop eating her food. She might have an upset tummy.

How long does the dog live for?

25

Getting old

A golden retriever can live until she is ten to twelve years old. When she is about eight years old, she might start to slow down.

This dog is too old to run around much.

An older dog spends more time asleep.

The dog gets older. She does not want
to go for long walks. She cannot see
or hear as well as before.

27

Life cycle of a dog

1
Puppy is born
(day 1)

2
Puppy feeds on
mother's milk

3
Puppy leaves
mother
(3 months old)

4
Fully-grown dog
(18 months)

5
Male and
female dogs
mate
(18 months
–3 years)

6
Female dog
has puppies

28

Dog map

eye

fur

nose

whiskers

ear

tail

paw

claws

Glossary

diseases illnesses

exercise walking and running

female a girl animal

glossy shiny

grooming licking and cleaning an animal's fur

injection medicine given with a needle

litter a group of puppies born together

male a boy animal

mammal an animal that feeds its babies on milk

mate when a male and female animal come together to produce babies

nutrients food an animal needs to grow

teat part of the mother's body that the puppy drinks milk through

vet doctor who looks after animals

More books to read

Life Cycle of a Dog, Angela Royston (Heinemann Library, 2000)

Nature's Patterns: Animal Life Cycles, Anita Ganeri (Heinemann Library, 2005)

Websites to visit

Visit these websites to find out more interesting facts about golden retrievers and their life cycles:

http://www.thegoldenretrieverclub.co.uk
http://www.rspca.org

Index

Titles in the *How Living Things Grow* series include:

Hardback   0 431 05079 1

Hardback   0 431 05072 4

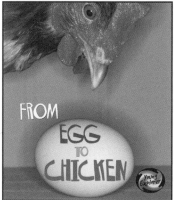

Hardback   0 431 05075 9

Hardback   0 431 05078 3

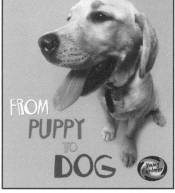

Hardback   0 431 05073 2

Hardback   0 431 05080 5

Hardback   0 431 05074 0

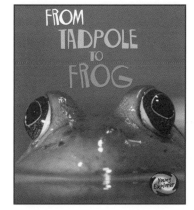

Hardback   0 431 05077 5

Find out about other Heinemann Library titles on our website www.heinemann.co.uk/library